MANVILLE

SOCCER SOURCE

WINNING BIG

WORLD AND EURO CUP SOCCER

Amanda Bishop

CRABTREE
Publishing Company
www.crabtreebooks.com

Author
Amanda Bishop

Publishing plan research and development
Kelly McNiven

Editors
Rachel Stuckey, Kelly McNiven

Proofreader and indexer
Natalie Hyde

Photo research
Melissa McClellan

Design
Tibor Choleva

Prepress technician
Margaret Amy Salter

Print and production coordinator
Margaret Amy Salter

Consultant
Sonja Cori Missio, International soccer correspondent, featured in The Guardian, Forza Italian Football, and Soccer Newsday

Photographs
Keystone Press: Marc Mueller (p 9 top); zumapress.com (p 9 bottom, p 10, p 12, p 18) Eduardo Maynard (p 29 left)
Corbis: Srdjan Suki/epa/Corbis (p 25 left); Thomas Eisenhuth/isiphotos.com (p 27 left)
SuperStock: © Jonathan Larsen (p 24, 25 right)
Associated Press: Hussein Malla (p 11 top)
Getty Images: Al Messerschmid (p 19); AFP (p 27 right); Stanley Chou/Stringer (p 29)
Shutterstock.com: © katatonia82 (front cover, p 21 bottom); © mooinblack (title page); © Iurii Osadchi (p 3); © fstockfoto (p 4); © spirit of america (p 5); © Maxisport (p 7); © photofriday (p 8–9 top); © Natursports (p 8–9 bottom); © Jaguar PS (p 11 bottom); © Martynova Anna (p 14); © Yiannis Kourtoglou (p 16 bottom); © Patryk Kosmider (p 16–17); © Tomasz Bidermann (p 17 bottom); © Vladimir Melnik (p 22–23 top, p 23 bottom); © jbor (p 22–23 bottom); © JBOY (p 28); © Jim Parkin (p 30)
Istockphoto: © eriktham (p 6)
© FIFA: p 23, p 29
© UEFA: p 20, p 21 top
Creative Commons License: © Marcello Casal Jr/ABr (p 15); © Reindertot (p 22 bottom); © Desconocido (p 26); © One95 (p 28–29 top)

Created for Crabtree Publishing by BlueApple*Works*

Cover: Spain's national football team celebrates after winning the UEFA EURO 2012 Championship against Italy in Kyiv, Ukraine.
Title page: Vinicius of Brazil holds the trophy after winning the 2012 FIFA Futsal World Cup Final in Bangkok, Thailand.

Library and Archives Canada Cataloguing in Publication

Bishop, Amanda, author
    Winning big : World and Euro Cup Soccer / Amanda Bishop.

(Soccer source)
Includes index.
Issued in print and electronic formats.
ISBN 978-0-7787-0245-0 (bound).--ISBN 978-0-7787-0253-5 (pbk.).--
ISBN 978-1-4271-9434-3 (pdf).--ISBN 978-1-4271-9430-5 (html)

        1. Soccer--Juvenile literature. 2. World Cup (Soccer)--Juvenile
literature. 3. European Championship (Soccer tournament)--
Juvenile literature. I. Title.

GV943.45.B58 2013   j796.334'66   C2013-905777-3
                                              C2013-905778-1

Library of Congress Cataloging-in-Publication Data

Bishop, Amanda.
  Soccer source winning big : World and Euro Cup soccer / Amanda Bishop.
       pages cm -- (Soccer Source)
  Includes index.
   ISBN 978-0-7787-0245-0 (reinforced library binding : alk. paper) -- ISBN 978-0-7787-0253-5 (pbk. : alk. paper) -- ISBN 978-1-4271-9434-3 (electronic pdf : alk. paper) -- ISBN 978-1-4271-9430-5 (electronic html : alk. paper)
 1. World Cup (Soccer)--Juvenile literature. I. Title.

  GV943.49.B53 2014
  796.334'66--dc23
                              2013033222

Crabtree Publishing Company

www.crabtreebooks.com   1-800-387-7650

Printed in Canada/092013/BF20130815

Published in Canada
Crabtree Publishing
616 Welland Ave.
St. Catharines, Ontario
L2M 5V6

Published in the United States
Crabtree Publishing
PMB 59051
350 Fifth Avenue, 59th Floor
New York, New York 10118

Published in the United Kingdom
Crabtree Publishing
Maritime House
Basin Road North, Hove
BN41 1WR

Published in Australia
Crabtree Publishing
3 Charles Street
Coburg North
VIC 3058

CONTENTS

THE BEAUTIFUL GAME

Soccer is the world's most popular sport. All you need to play is a ball, two pairs of **goal** markers, and a few friends. Most people play for fun and exercise. The best players in the world compete in **international tournaments** such as the Olympics, the UEFA European Championship, and the FIFA World Cup.

A Global Phenomenon

The modern game of soccer was first played in the 1800s at public schools in England. It quickly became a **national** pastime. English sailors who spent months at sea would jump at the chance to play a quick **match**, or game, of "football" when they went ashore in other countries. Local people in these countries saw them playing and began to play themselves. Soccer soon spread around the world.

Wayne Rooney has played for the English national team since 2003.

4

Getting In On the Action

You may play soccer at your school or in a local **league**. **Professional** players, or players who are paid to play, usually belong to soccer **clubs**. Club teams compete in regional or national leagues, such as the National Women's Soccer League (NWSL) in the United States or the English Premier League (EPL) in England. The top players in each country often play for their national teams, too.

With a little imagination, soccer can be played anywhere. The children on the right are using an empty water bottle as a ball.

Soccer vs. Football

American football grew out of soccer and **rugby**. In other parts of the world, however, soccer is known as football. The following terms are sometimes used outside of North America and Australia in relation to soccer.

North America And Australia	International
soccer	football
field	pitch
team	side or squad
game	match
uniform	kit
cleats	boots
tie	draw

WHO MAKES THE RULES?

The **Fédération Internationale de Football Association (FIFA)** is a **federation** of national soccer associations. The member associations of FIFA all agree to play soccer using the same **regulations**, or rules. FIFA also organizes international tournaments such as the World Cup.

The Rules of the Game

The **Laws of the Game**, or the official rules of soccer, are decided by the **International Football Association Board (IFAB)**. As modern soccer originated in Great Britain, the IFAB is made up of the English, Scottish, Welsh, and Northern Irish football associations, plus four representatives from FIFA. In order to change any rule, the members of IFAB must vote. Two-thirds of the votes are required to make any changes to the rules.

FIFA headquarters are located in Zurich, Switzerland.

Making the Right Call

The **referee** enforces the rules of the game. He or she awards a goal only if the entire ball crosses the **goal line**. In 2012, the IFAB approved the use of **goal-line technology**. FIFA has announced goal-line technology will be used at the 2014 World Cup in Brazil.

FIFA represents soccer associations from over 200 countries.

How Goal-Line Technology Works

In one type of goal-line technology, several cameras are focused on each goal to track the ball's movement.

The cameras continually track the ball, sending signals to a computer to show the ball's exact location.

When a team scores, the computer sends a radio signal to a wristwatch worn by the referee. The watch shows the word "GOAL." The referee, however, makes the final decision about whether or not a goal has been scored.

This special watch helps the referee to fairly enforce the rules of the game.

COMPETING ON THE WORLD STAGE

Soccer's global popularity makes international tournaments very exciting! Competitions bring together players from all over the world. Some events are for youth, such as **U-17 tournaments** for boys and girls under the age of seventeen. Others are for certain types of soccer, such as beach soccer or **futsal**, a kind of indoor soccer.

Futsal stadium

A Global Game

Players from all over the world show off their skills in international competition. The best players are often **recruited**, or invited, to play for club teams in countries other than their home country. These players may then play against their club teammates while competing for their national team.

Did You Know?

Kristine Lilly of the United States has the most international **caps**, or appearances on the national team, in the history of soccer.

The annual Homeless World Cup brings together homeless players from 70 countries to experience the joy of the game together.

Confederation Tournaments

FIFA's six **continental confederations** each host tournaments for their member teams. A **qualifying event** decides which teams move on to the next level of competition. The Confederations Cup is held every four years. Eight teams compete for this title, including the top team from each confederation, the World Cup champions, and a team from the host country.

AFC - represents Asian nations

CAF - represents African nations

CONCACAF - represents North American, Central American, and Caribbean nations

CONMEBOL - represents South American nations

OFC - represents Oceanian nations

UEFA - represents European nations

In 2013, host country Brazil won their third straight Confederations Cup.

OLYMPIC MEN'S SOCCER

Soccer became an official part of the Olympics at the 1908 London games. With eight teams competing, it was the first team sport to be included in the Olympics. In the final match, Great Britain beat Denmark 2-0 to win the first gold medal in soccer.

London 2012

The Olympics were held in London again in 2012. This time, 16 men's teams in four groups competed in the tournament. The top two teams from each group advanced to the quarter-finals. The winners of those games played semi-final matches. The two semi-final winners, Mexico and Brazil, played for the gold. The two losing teams, South Korea and Japan, battled for the bronze. In the end, Mexico captured the gold medal, Brazil won the silver, and South Korea earned the bronze.

This picture shows Brazil's Neymar (right) in action against Jorge Enriquez of Mexico during the gold-medal match at the 2012 London Olympics.

Leveling the Field

In 1984, Olympic regulations allowed professional players to compete. Since most of the world's top soccer players were from Europe and South America, FIFA adjusted the rules to make the game as fair as possible. FIFA stops any player from UEFA or CONMEBOL who has appeared in a World Cup game from playing at the Olympics.

A men's Olympic soccer team can include 18 players, but only three of them can be over the age of 23.

Mexico beat Brazil 2-1 to win the country's first gold medal in soccer at the 2012 Summer Olympics.

This picture shows the gold medal awarded at the 2012 London Olympics.

Women's soccer became an official Olympic sport at the 1996 Olympics in Atlanta, Georgia. The top eight teams from the 1995 Women's World Cup qualified for the tournament and played a total of sixteen games. The United States beat China to win the gold medal and Norway defeated Brazil for the bronze.

Qualifying Tournaments

To qualify for the Olympics, most teams compete in tournaments hosted by FIFA's continental confederations. Only UEFA does not hold a qualifying tournament. Instead, it sends the top European teams from the Women's World Cup. One place is always reserved for the host nation, so Brazil will qualify automatically for the Olympics in Rio de Janeiro in 2016.

Canadian team captain Christine Sinclair celebrates after scoring the second goal for Canada during the 2012 Olympic quarter-final game against Great Britain.

Getting Onside with Women's Soccer

After 88 years of men's Olympic soccer, women's teams were finally allowed to compete at the Olympic Games. Soccer has been played by women for over a hundred years, but opportunities for women to play on the world stage were rare until recently. A growing popularity in women's international soccer and women's leagues shows that the sport has a promising future.

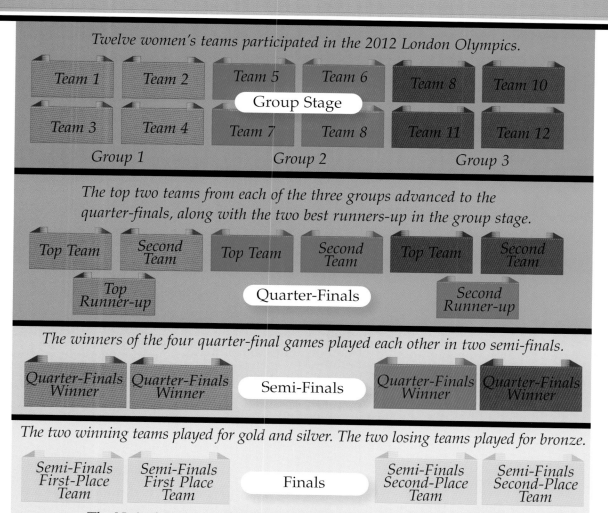

Twelve women's teams participated in the 2012 London Olympics.

Team 1	Team 2	Team 5	Team 6	Team 8	Team 10
Team 3	Team 4	Team 7	Team 8	Team 11	Team 12

Group Stage

Group 1   Group 2   Group 3

The top two teams from each of the three groups advanced to the quarter-finals, along with the two best runners-up in the group stage.

| Top Team | Second Team | Top Team | Second Team | Top Team | Second Team |

Top Runner-up   Quarter-Finals   Second Runner-up

The winners of the four quarter-final games played each other in two semi-finals.

| Quarter-Finals Winner | Quarter-Finals Winner | Semi-Finals | Quarter-Finals Winner | Quarter-Finals Winner |

The two winning teams played for gold and silver. The two losing teams played for bronze.

| Semi-Finals First-Place Team | Semi-Finals First Place Team | Finals | Semi-Finals Second-Place Team | Semi-Finals Second-Place Team |

The United States won their third straight Olympic gold medal, with Japan taking silver. Canada defeated France to win the bronze.

PARALYMPIC SOCCER

The Paralympic Games are an international competition for athletes with physical or intellectual **disabilities**. The most recent Paralympic Games were held in London in 2012, not long after the Olympics finished. They featured two forms of soccer. Five-a-side and seven-a-side soccer both use FIFA rules that have been adapted to the needs of the players.

Seven-a-Side Soccer

Seven-a-side soccer has been part of the Paralympic Games since 1984. Athletes with **muscular impairments** resulting from **cerebral palsy**, strokes, or brain injuries, play seven-a-side. Each player falls into one of four categories, depending on his or her level of impairment. Teams must have at least one athlete in the most severely impaired categories on the field, or else remove one of their players, to ensure the teams are evenly matched.

Seven-a-side soccer allows one-handed throw-ins and eliminates the offside rule.

Five-a-Side Soccer

Five-a-side soccer is played by athletes who are **visually impaired**. It was added to the Summer Paralympic Games in 2004. The goaltender can be fully sighted, but the other four players must wear blindfolds to make sure that they all have the same level of visual impairment. The ball makes a sound to help the players keep track of it. Teams also use two guides, who stand off the field and call out directions to the players.

The Cerebral Palsy International Sports and Recreation Association organized the first international seven-a-side competition in Scotland in 1978.

The International Blind Sports Federation organizes world championships and youth championships for five-a-side soccer.

THE EURO CUP

The men's and women's Euros are hosted by UEFA. These action-packed tournaments pit the best European teams against one another. The summer events also give European league fans a chance to watch their favorite players in the off-season!

A Changing Tradition

The first Euro, called the UEFA European Nations Cup, was held in 1960 in France. By 1980, the number of teams had increased from four to eight. In 1996, the tournament grew to 16 teams. The 16 teams in the 2012 tournament qualified from a group of 51 teams. The qualifying games began in August of 2010 and continued until the finalists were decided in November of 2011. The qualification process can take up to two years to complete, so it starts soon after the World Cup finishes.

Spanish forward Fernando Torres scored goals in both the 2008 and 2012 finals, making him the only player to have scored in two final games at the Euro.

Women's Euro 2013

The first Women's Euro was held in 1991 with four teams in competition. By July 2013, the Women's Euro had expanded to twelve teams. The spectacular 2013 event set records in attendance. One of the biggest surprises was the Danish team, which made it all the way to the semi-finals without winning a game in regular time! In the end, Germany took home the gold medal after defeating Norway. Over 41,000 fans cheered on their teams at the final game!

As host nations, Poland and Ukraine automatically qualified for the Men's Euro in 2012. It was Ukraine's first appearance at the tournament, and Poland's second appearance.

Did You Know?

In 1984, the Euro stopped playing games to decide third place, as is done in the Olympics and the World Cup.

GREAT EURO MOMENTS

Euro tournaments showcase some of the best players in the world. It is no surprise that there are some heart-stopping moments! Some involve amazing individual plays. Others are **feats** that could only be achieved through teamwork.

Euro 92

The men's team from Denmark did not even qualify for the Euro in 1992. They were added only after Yugoslavia had to leave the tournament. Denmark surprised everyone by beating the Netherlands in penalty kicks to win the semi-final game. When Denmark defeated Germany to win the Cup, sports fans all over Europe could barely believe it!

*German striker Oliver Bierhoff (front) scores the **golden goal** at the Euro 96 final. IFAB dropped the golden goal from the Laws of the Game in 2004.*

Euro 96

In 1993, FIFA introduced the rule of the golden goal, or the first goal scored in overtime to immediately end the game. The Euro 96 was the first to allow the golden goal. In the final match between Germany and the Czech Republic, Oliver Bierhoff leveled the score at 1-1 during regular time. Then, in the fifth minute of extra time, or the overtime period, he scored again to win and end the game. His was the first golden goal scored in a major tournament.

Women's Euro 97

Norwegian striker Marianne Pettersen first played for her national team in 1994. She later scored one of the two goals that led Norway to victory over Germany in the 1995 Women's World Cup. But in Norway's opening game against Denmark at the Women's Euro 97, Pettersen scored a whopping four of the team's five goals to beat Denmark 5-0! Norway did not advance out of the group stage, but it was an unforgettable performance from a top player.

Marianne Pettersen scored 66 goals in 98 international matches.

THE NEXT EUROS

Both the men's and women's Euro take place every four years. They always fall two years after the World Cup is played. The timing of these events means that soccer fans always have a major international tournament to cheer for!

Euro 2016

France will host the next Euro in 2016 at ten different stadiums across the country. For the first time, there will be 24 teams competing in the final tournament instead of 16. France will qualify automatically, but more than 50 other teams will play for their spots between September 2014 and November 2015. There will likely be some teams making their first appearance in the Euro, which will add to the excitement. The final groups will be announced in December of 2015. The winner of Euro 2016 secures a spot in the 2017 Confederations Cup, which will be held in Russia.

The official logo of the 2016 Euro

Women's Euro 2017

The Women's Euro is also growing. When the next Euro is played in 2017, 16 teams will participate instead of twelve. The host country (or countries) will likely be decided in 2014. Before Sweden was awarded the 2013 tournament, the Netherlands, Poland, Bulgaria, and Switzerland all expressed an interest in hosting. Perhaps the next Women's Euro will be in one of these countries!

A replica, or copy, of the trophy for the men's 2016 Euro is on display in Paris, France.

The Spanish national team won the Euro Cup in 2012. Sports fans around the world will be excited to watch the team play again in 2016!

THE FIFA WORLD CUP

The FIFA World Cup is one of the most anticipated sporting events on the international scene. Every four years, soccer fans gather to watch the world's best national teams take each other on. There may be as many tears as there are cheers, but no one seems to mind!

The First World Cup

Uruguay hosted the first World Cup in 1930. Teams were invited to play, instead of qualifying as they do today. Only four teams from Europe agreed to go, because sailing to South America for the tournament required teams to be away from home for more than two months! The final number of participating teams was 13. When Uruguay beat Argentina in the final match to win the very first Cup, a national holiday was declared!

The Jules Rimet Trophy was awarded to the World Cup winner until it was permanently given to Brazil in 1970 after their third World Cup victory. It was stolen in 1983 and never found.

World Cup 2010

The 2010 World Cup was hosted by South Africa. In 2007, 204 men's teams began competing to qualify for one of the 32 available spots. Each of the 32 qualifiers received one million dollars from FIFA to help pay for training in preparation for the tournament. Teams were also awarded prize money. The winning country, Spain, received $30 million in addition to the Cup! Spain defeated the Netherlands 1-0 to win, and Germany beat Uruguay 3-2 in the third-place game.

Zakumi was the mascot for the 2010 World Cup. The 2010 World Cup was the first to be held in Africa.

At the end of the 2010 World Cup, closing ceremonies were held before the final match between Spain and the Netherlands.

Did You Know?
The most common score in a World Cup final match is 1-0.

THE FIFA WOMEN'S WORLD CUP

In 1991, China hosted the first FIFA Women's World Cup. National teams from 49 countries competed to make the top twelve and play in the final tournament. The United States defeated Norway 2-1 for the Cup, and Sweden beat Germany 4-0 in the third-place game.

Women's World Cup 2011

To qualify for the 2011 Women's World Cup, teams battled it out in continental confederation tournaments. The top sixteen teams headed to Germany for the final tournament. They played a group stage, quarter-finals, and semi-finals before the final. Japan became the first Asian team to win a World Cup, beating the United States in a shoot-out.

Japanese team captain Homare Sawa holds the World Cup trophy after Japan defeated the United States in the FIFA Women's World Cup.

At the 1991 Women's World Cup, the players were not the only history-makers on the field. For the first time in FIFA history, female officials took to the fields to call the shots!

The United States Women's Team

The United States women's team has long been a leader in international soccer. After winning the first Women's World Cup in 1991, they won again in 1999, won the third-place games in 2003 and 2007, and were runners-up to Japan at the last tournament. They also hold four Olympic gold medals and have won the **Algarve Cup** nine times to date!

American goaltender Hope Solo won the Golden Glove Award for top keeper of the tournament in 2011.

*At the 2007 Women's World Cup, German goaltender Nadine Angerer had five **shut-outs** in a row. Germany won the tournament and did not allow a single goal!*

Almost every soccer fan has a favorite World Cup moment. At the first tournament in Uruguay in 1930, Uruguayan player Héctor Castro inspired the world. Castro had lost his arm when he was only 13, but it did not stop him from playing soccer. He went on to score Uruguay's first goal as well as the last goal in the final, winning the first World Cup for the host country. Since then, the World Cup has seen many more amazing achievements.

Héctor Castro

World Cup 1990

The first African team to make it to the World Cup was Egypt in 1934. Then the world had to wait until 1970 to see another African team play in the tournament. In 1986, Morocco became the first African team to make it to the second round. Then, in 1990, Roger Milla of Cameroon made a brilliant steal from his Colombian opponent during extra time in a group-stage game. He brought the ball down the field and scored. Cameroon won the match and became the first African team to make it to the quarter-finals.

Women's World Cup 2011

In the quarter-finals of the 2011 Women's World Cup, the United States and Brazil went to extra time after ending 90 minutes in a tie. At 120 minutes, Brazil was leading 2-1. Then, in the second minute of **added time**, American forward Abby Wambach headed in an incredible goal. The resulting tie sent the two teams to penalty kicks, and United States won with five goals to Brazil's three.

In 2010, for the first time in World Cup history, a team included three brothers—the Palacios brothers of Honduras.

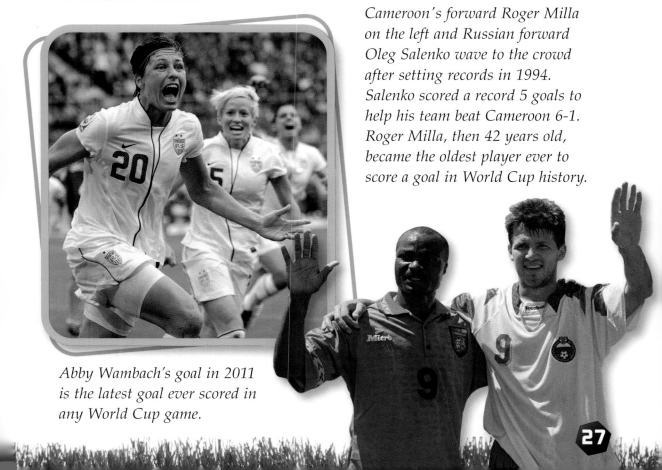

Cameroon's forward Roger Milla on the left and Russian forward Oleg Salenko wave to the crowd after setting records in 1994. Salenko scored a record 5 goals to help his team beat Cameroon 6-1. Roger Milla, then 42 years old, became the oldest player ever to score a goal in World Cup history.

Abby Wambach's goal in 2011 is the latest goal ever scored in any World Cup game.

WORLD CUPS COMING UP!

Soccer fans do not have much longer to wait for World Cup action! The next men's tournament is in Brazil in 2014. A year later, in 2015, the women will kick off in Canada.

The Road to Rio

In June of 2013, giant countdown clocks were unveiled in the Brazilian cities of Rio de Janeiro, Brasilia, and Sao Paulo. The clocks will help local fans keep track of how many days, hours, and minutes are left before the next World Cup begins on June 12, 2014. Brazil has won the World Cup more times than any other country. However, the last time Brazil hosted the tournament in 1950, they lost in the final to Uruguay. In 2014, the whole country is hoping for a win on home soil!

The 2014 World Cup will be held in twelve cities around Brazil.

CANADA
2015
FIFA
WOMEN'S WORLD CUP

Soccer Strong and Free

Canada's first Women's World Cup will run from June 6 to July 5, 2015. The games will be played in six cities from coast to coast. For the first time, 24 teams will compete for the title. Key rivalries to watch for include the home team and their southern neighbors, the United States. After a controversial semi-final match at the 2012 Olympics, both teams are ready to play again at the 2015 World Cup.

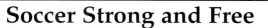

Background image: A soccer stadium in Vancouver, British Columbia is one of the six fields teams will compete on in the 2015 Women's World Cup.

2014 FIFA World Cup Brazil

Canada's women's team poses for a team picture before their 2012 Olympic semi-final game against the United States.

Did You Know?

Fuleco the armadillo is the mascot for the 2014 World Cup. Mascots have been a part of the World Cup tradition since 1966.

29

Will you be playing in the next World Cup? It is easy to get started! Find a ball, a friend or two, and a safe place to start practicing your moves.

Team Spirit, School Spirit

Many schools have soccer teams. School teams usually have a lot of fans at the school. Cheering for the team is also a lot of fun! Joining your school team is a great way to learn the sport.

Youth leagues offer an opportunity to train over the summer.

LEARNING MORE

Books

Gifford, Clive. *Soccer World Cup*. Crabtree Publishing, 2009.

Horby, Hugh. *Eyewitness Soccer*. Dorling Kindersley, 2010.

Whitfield, David. *World Cup*. Weigl AV2, 2013.

Web Sites

FIFA

FIFA's web site is a terrific place to find out about world soccer players and events.

www.fifa.com

U.S. Youth Soccer

This site has information for players, parents, and coaches about how to get involved in the soccer community.

www.usyouthsoccer.org

U.S. Soccer

The United States national soccer web site is a great resource for following the U.S. national men's and women's soccer teams and your favorite players.

www.ussoccer.com

Canadian Soccer Association

Canada's national soccer site can help you keep track of the men's and women's national teams and your favorite players.

www.canadasoccer.com

GLOSSARY

Note: Some boldfaced words are defined where they appear in the book.

added time Time added to the end of a period to make up for any minutes not played in regular time due to injuries or other breaks in play

Algarve Cup An annual women's tournament featuring the best women's teams from around the world

cerebral palsy A physical condition that causes difficulty in body movement

club A soccer organization that has one or more teams, which compete in a regional or national league

continental confederation An organization of the national soccer associations on one continent

disabilities Conditions that may limit one's activities

feats An act of achievement, usually involving skill or strength

federation A collection of organizations that work together

goal A point scored when the ball enters the net; also used to refer to the net

goal line The line across the front of the net

International Football Association Board (IFAB) The organization responsible for deciding the rules of the game

international tournament A series of games played by national teams over a set period of time

league A group of clubs that play against one another

muscular impairment A disability relating to muscles or movement

national Describes something related to one country

penalty shoot-out A series of penalty kicks at the end of a game taken by each team to break a tie

qualifying event A game or series of games that is played to determine who will move on to another tournament

quarter-final A series of four games played by the top eight teams in a tournament

rugby A game related to soccer in which one is allowed to use one's hands

semi-final A series of two games played by the top four teams in a tournament

visually impaired Describes a condition of limited or no eyesight

INDEX